**Matthew**

C000069961

# Prevailing

# Prayer

## *Against Spirits of Wickedness*

# 700

### PRAYER POINTS

### Against Satanic Delays, Witchcraft,

### Fear, Barriers and Setbacks

© 2001 Matthew Ashimolowo

Published by Mattyson Media an imprint of MAMM
Matthew Ashimolowo Media Ministries
57 Waterden Road
Hackney Wick
London
E15 2EE

ISBN  1 - 874 - 646 - 51 -1

Bible quotes are from the King James Bible
unless otherwise stated.

Printed in England by Clays Plc

# Contents

# THE SPIRIT OF SABOTEUR

1.     Come against the spirit that want to sabotage your destiny

2.     Send the fire of God against anything that turns the glory of God in your life to shame - Psalms 4:2

> O ye sons of men, how long will ye turn my glory into shame? how long will ye love vanity, and seek after leasing? Selah.
> Psalms 4:2 (KJV)

3.     Release the fire of God against those who want to nullify good things in your life

4.  Celebrate the departure of those who must go for you to grow in the name of Jesus

5.  Every evil planting; the Cains, the Esaus, the Judases that are in your company - command them to be scattered in the name of the Lord

6.  Begin to release all the favour of blessing and goodness of the Lord that has been tied down by the spirit of wickedness

7.  Pray for divine insight and the gift of the discerning of spirits to expose anything operating around you

8.  Take authority over the enemy who has confiscated your blessing and begin to take it back in the name of the Lord

9.  Those who are perpetrators of evil counsel - the Lord will frustrate their counselling

10.  Thank God because your agreement with hell shall not stand because you are bound for heaven

11.  Declare that every attempt to malign your name will be exposed by the Lord

12.  Thank the Lord because He will cause your faithfulness and your faith to speak for you in Jesus name

13.    Take authority over every tongue that wants to speak against your peace even before they start and declare that their words shall fall and die

14.    Boldly declare that you are willing and obedient, you will eat the best of the land - Isaiah 1:19

> If ye be willing and obedient, ye shall eat the good of the land:
> Isaiah 1:19 (KJV)

15.    Release ministering angels to pursue everyone holding what belongs to you that they begin to cough it up in Jesus name

16.    Thank God because He has ordained you to enjoy everything that pertains to life and godliness

17.    Begin to decree that God will frustrate all their works and weapons

18.    Take back every of your property which the enemy is trying to divert in the name of the Lord

19.    Declare your authority over every spirit that is diverting the benefits belonging to you

20.    Boldly declare that you would not build for other people to occupy

21.    Declare that every plan to shift you from the place of God's planting would meet with frustration

22.    Ask  Lord to expose every transfer on movement which is not orchestrated by Him

23.    Pray that any relocation that would result in destruction for you or your family would be exposed by the Lord Ruth 1:1-3, 5

Now it came to pass in the days when the judges ruled, that there was a famine in the land. And a certain man of Bethlehemjudah went to sojourn in the country of Moab, he, and his wife, and his two sons.  And the name of the man was Elimelech, and the name of his wife Naomi, and the name of his two sons Mahlon and Chilion, Ephrathites of Bethlehemjudah. And they came into the country of Moab, and continued there. And Elimelech Naomi's husband died; and she was left, and her two sons.

And Mahlon and Chilion died also both of them; and the woman was left of her two sons and her husband.
Ruth 1:1-3, 5 (KJV)

24.    Receive boldness to overcome every roaring lion that has vowed to devour you

25.    Ask the Lord to expose everyone who is carrying the spirit of Absalom and trying to conspire against you - 2 Samuel 15 - 18

26.    Thank God because He has made Himself an enemy of your enemies

27.    Plead the blood of Jesus against every instrument of wickedness that has been raised against you - Revelation 12:11

And they overcame him by the blood of the Lamb, and by the word of their testimony; and they loved not their lives unto the death.
Revelation 12:11 (KJV)

28.    Come against the spirit of wickedness that is trying to destroy the peace and tranquillity you enjoy at home and work -
Psalms 2:2-4

The kings of the earth set themselves, and the rulers take counsel together, against the LORD, and against his anointed, saying, Let us break their bands asunder, and cast away their cords from us. He that sitteth in the heavens shall laugh: the Lord shall have them
in derision.
Psalms 2:2-4 (KJV)

29.    Pray that every terror planned to destroy and devastate you shall not work in the name of Jesus

30.    Come against every satanic attempt to sabotage your future

31.     I command a straightening out to everything the enemy has made crooked - Isaiah 45:2

32.     Decree that the seed the enemy has sown shall not bear fruit

33.     Declare and decree that those who only see evil in all that you are doing will be embarrassed and put to shame

34.     Every spirit assigned to sabotage your vision and destiny will be put to shame in the name of Jesus

35.     Reject every attempt of the enemy to discredit and despise your assignment

36.     Bring the fire of God against a sabotaged spirit that wants to make you a person of mockery

37.     Thank God because the dreams and visions He has put in you will never be stopped

38.     Pray that those who are aggrieved because of your vision would be put to shame - Nehemiah 2:10
When Sanballat the Horonite, and Tobiah the servant, the Ammonite, heard of it, it grieved them exceedingly that there was come a man to seek the welfare of the children of Israel.
Nehemiah 2:10 (KJV)

39.    Ask the Lord to expose those who are exposers of good things around you

40.    Ask the Lord to expose the heart of those who are calling your good deeds evil

41.    Declare and decree that no weapon of the enemy released to sabotage, destroy or stop you will work

42.    Ask the Lord to open your eyes that you may know every agent of satan walking around you

43.    Release God's fire against every "toiling spirit" that is plaguing your life

44.    Boldly declare that you have received the anointing to become unstoppable by the enemy

45.    Bring the fire of God against every vision killer

46.    Release the fire of God against every spirit that is trying to use blackmail to destroy my career

47.    I release the fire of God against every attempt of the enemy to frustrate my spiritual destiny

48.    Bring the fire of God against every dragon spirit ready to devour your vision - Revelation 12:4

And his tail drew the third part of the stars of heaven, and did cast them to the earth: and the dragon stood

before the woman which was ready to be delivered, for
to devour her child as soon as it was born.
Revelation 12:4 (KJV)

49.    Ask the Lord to expose to you those who are
trying to malign you with the intention of taking your
blessing


50.    I receive God's immunity from every attack of
what belongs to me


51.    Lay hands on all that belongs to you and begin to
call favour upon it

# THE SPIRIT OF INTIMIDATION, MANIPULATION & CONTROL

1.　Break the grip of every satanic intimidation over your life in the name of Jesus

2.　Pray that those who have made themselves instruments of oppression shall be put to shame in your life

3.    Receive the boldness of the Lord and declare yourself free from fear of the enemy - Deuteronomy 1:29

> Then I said unto you, Dread not, neither be afraid of them.
> Deuteronomy 1:29 (KJV)

4.    Cast out every demonic force that has entered the territory of your life

5.    Boldly declare that you are above satanic control

6.    Pray that satan's weapon of fear will be frustrated by the Lord

7.    Declare that there shall be embarrassment for those who covet God's promotion in your life

8.    Pray that every false accusation brought against you will be embarrassed and put to shame

9.    Declare that all those who are manipulating your destiny will be put to shame

10.    Every spirit trying to manipulate my circumstance will be frustrated in Jesus name

11.    Every attempt of the enemy to manipulate the battles I am facing will experience frustration in the name of the Lord

12.    You spirits of manipulation, the fire of God is against you

13.    Anybody wanting to use me for their own inordinate gains, their plans will come to frustration

14.    Reject the spirit of fear and intimidation which is intended to bind you

15.    Bind the power and control of the spirit of fear over your life - Nehemiah 6:12

> And, lo, I perceived that God had not sent him; but that he pronounced this prophecy against me: for Tobiah and Sanballat had hired him.
> Nehemiah 6:12 (KJV)

16.    Decree that every spell meant for your misfortune or failure will turn around for the opposite

17.    Decree that every spell meant for operation, bondage and exploitation in your life will turn around for the opposite

18.    Declare and decree that everyone misusing their exalted and anointed position to attack you, that their attack shall not stand - Deuteronomy 23:5

> Nevertheless the LORD thy God would not hearken unto Balaam; but the LORD thy God turned the curse into a blessing unto thee, because the LORD thy God loved thee.
> Deuteronomy 23:5 (KJV)

19.     Bring the fire of God against any Absalom spirit that divides the family

20.     Break yourself free from the spirit of the fear of man like Saul had

21.     Bind every suicide spirit that is trying to control your mind in the name of the Lord -1 Samuel 15:27-28

And as Samuel turned about to go away, he laid hold upon the skirt of his mantle, and it rent.
And Samuel said unto him, The LORD hath rent the kingdom of Israel from thee this day, and hath given it to a neighbour of thine, that is better than thou.
1 Samuel 15:27-28 (KJV)

22.     Boldly declare to every Jezebel spirit that you shall not be intimidated

23.     Loose yourself from the grip of the spirit of fear - 2 Timothy 1:7

For God hath not given us the spirit of fear; but of power, and of love, and of a sound mind.
2 Timothy 1:7 (KJV)

24.     Declare that every attempt of the enemy to make you afraid shall not work

# THE SPIRIT OF RAGS, COVERING & GRAVE CLOTHES

1.   Bind every spirit that wants to convert your prosperity to poverty

2.   Declare that God will frustrate the effort of Herods who want to kill you - Acts 12:1-5

Now about that time Herod the king stretched forth his hands to vex certain of the church. And he killed James the brother of John with the sword. And because he saw it pleased the Jews, he proceeded further to take Peter also. (Then were the days of unleavened bread.) And when he had apprehended him, he put him in prison, and delivered him to four quaternions of soldiers to keep him; intending after Easter to bring him forth to the people. Peter therefore was kept in prison: but prayer was made without ceasing of the church unto God for him.

Acts 12:1-5 (KJV)

3. Prophesy that those who are digging a pit for your destruction shall fall into it themselves

4. Prophesy that every evil that seeks your life shall die for your sake

5. Send every spirit of poverty, lack and penury permanently to the bottomless pit of hell and proclaim that there will be no peace for every son of wickedness that comes against me

6. Every devourer of money, visible and invisible in my life are stopped from henceforth in Jesus name

7. Boldly declare that your covenant with early death is broken in the name of Jesus - Isaiah 28:18

And your covenant with death shall be disannulled, and your agreement with hell shall not stand; when the overflowing scourge shall pass through, then ye shall be trodden down by it.

Isaiah 28:18 (KJV)

8.    I tear satan's garment of wretchedness

9.    I reject every picture, every image of poverty, wretchedness and retardation which the enemy is painting about me

10.    Pray for the boldness to be alert and awake in the spirit

11.    Boldly proclaim that poverty and wretchedness is not your portion

12.    Receive the miracle that will move you from broke to breakthrough

13.    Saul rented the garment of Samuel - pray for the grace to not touch the anointed of God

14.    Receive boldness to lift your head and not bow in sorrow in Jesus name

15.    Lay hands on all that belongs to you and proclaim that there shall be no loss - Acts 27:22

And now I exhort you to be of good cheer: for there shall be no loss of any man's life among you, but of the ship.
Acts 27:22 (KJV)

16.    Declare that the Son of God has set you free and you refuse to be bound

17.    Declare that every spirit of destruction shall meet with destruction - Psalms 52:5

God shall likewise destroy thee for ever, he shall take thee away, and pluck thee out of thy dwelling place, and root thee out of the land of the living. Selah.
Psalms 52:5 (KJV)

# THE SPIRIT OF RESISTANCE

1.    Tear down every satanic blackmail

2.    Take authority over every spirit of oppression and conspiracy

3.    Break every chain and bond with which the wicked have tied you down

4.    Declare that every wickedness proceeding from the wicked shall return to sender - 1 Samuel 24:13

As saith the proverb of the ancients, Wickedness proceedeth from the wicked: but mine hand shall not

be upon thee.
1 Samuel 24:13 (KJV)

5.     Declare that you refuse to permit any witch or witchcraft to stay alive - Exodus 22:18

Thou shalt not suffer a witch to live.
Exodus 22:18 (KJV)

6.     Those who conspired against Paul died of their own harm - boldly declare that that is the portion of every attack of the wicked in your life - Acts 23:13

And they were more than forty which had made this conspiracy.
Acts 23:13 (KJV)

7.     Pray that the favour of the Lord will be so manifest in your life that it will silence the opposition - Ecclesiastes 3:13

And also that every man should eat and drink, and enjoy the good of all his labour, it is the gift of God.
Ecclesiastes 3:13 (KJV)

8.     Prophesy that every evil imagined and plotted against you will turn around for your good - Genesis 50:20

But as for you, ye thought evil against me; but God
meant it unto good, to bring to pass, as it is this day, to
save much people alive.
Genesis 50:20 (KJV)

9.     May the angel of the Lord pursue all those who
have gathered against my peace

10.     Thank God for clothing you with the spirit of
dread and fear in the heart of the enemy - Deuteronomy
2:25

This day will I begin to put the dread of thee and the
fear of thee upon the nations that are under the whole
heaven, who shall hear report of thee, and shall
tremble, and be in anguish because of thee.
Deuteronomy 2:25 (KJV)

11.     My unique prophetic destiny shall come to pass
irrespective of all opposition

12.     Ask the Lord to contend with them who are
contending with you - Isaiah 49:25-26

But thus saith the LORD, Even the captives of the
mighty shall be taken away, and the prey of the terrible
shall be delivered: for I will contend with him that
contendeth with thee, and I will save thy children. And
I will feed them that oppress thee with their own flesh;
and they shall be drunken with their own blood, as with

sweet wine: and all flesh shall know that I the LORD am thy Saviour and thy Redeemer, the mighty One of Jacob.
Isaiah 49:25-26 (KJV)

13.     Thank God for redeeming you from generational family, and legal curse - Galatians 3:13

Christ hath redeemed us from the curse of the law, being made a curse for us: for it is written, Cursed is every one that hangeth on a tree:
Galatians 3:13 (KJV)

14.     Take authority over every spirit of wickedness and wicked forces that are at work right now in your life and break their grip

15.     Command the spirit of dumbness and deafness that does not want to let go to get away permanently from your life

16.     Exercise your God-given authority and destroy the weapons they are using against you

17.     Come against every spirit of jealousy that opposes you at every turn

18.     Boldly declare that you are too much for satan in the name of the Lord

19.     Go into the realm of the spirit and cut every tongue that is contrary to your progress - Exodus 11:7

But against any of the children of Israel shall not a dog move his tongue, against man or beast: that ye may know how that the LORD doth put a difference between the Egyptians and Israel.
Exodus 11:7 (KJV)

20.     Release ministering angels to go ahead of you and change every negative impression that has been created by perpetrators of evil

21.     Thank God because His decree shall be manifest in your life and none can stop it

22.     Begin to decree that the enemy's power shall be broken to pieces

23.     Pray that those who are trying to frustrate you because you frustrate their illegal activities will be exposed by the Lord

24.     Declare boldly that because you are the planting of the Lord you shall be unmoveable by the enemy

25.     Release God's fire against every plan of satan intended for your hurt and demobilisation

26.     Declare that you receive the spirit of sobriety and

vigilance to fight the enemy

27.     Release God's fire that will silence the adversary

28.     Send the fire of God into every camp of unholy alliance gathered against you - Numbers 16:8-11

And Moses said unto Korah, Hear, I pray you, ye sons of Levi: Seemeth it but a small thing unto you, that the God of Israel hath separated you from the congregation of Israel, to bring you near to himself to do the service of the tabernacle of the LORD, and to stand before the congregation to minister unto them? And he hath brought thee near to him, and all thy brethren the sons of Levi with thee: and seek ye the priesthood also? For which cause both thou and all thy company are gathered together against the LORD: and what is Aaron, that ye murmur against him?
Numbers 16:8-11 (KJV)

29.     Declare that in the midst of the battle, the hand of God, and the mark of His presence will be seen in your life - Numbers 16:28-30

And Moses said, Hereby ye shall know that the LORD hath sent me to do all these works; for I have not done them of mine own mind. If these men die the common death of all men, or if they be visited after the visitation of all men; then the LORD hath not sent me. But if the LORD make a new thing, and the earth open her mouth, and swallow them up, with all that

appertain unto them, and they go down quick into the pit; then ye shall understand that these men have provoked the LORD.
Numbers 16:28-30 (KJV)

30. Declare boldly that in the midst of every opposition, the glory of the Lord will be revealed in your life

31. Thank God because everyone who is conniving together to bring you down will be embarrassed and be put to shame

32. Every demonic entity that is attacking your peace and joy is sent back to hell's captivity in the name of Jesus

33. Bless the name of Jesus because whatever has chosen to stand against you is standing against the Lord - Exodus 23:22; Jeremiah 30:16

But if thou shalt indeed obey his voice, and do all that I speak; then I will be an enemy unto thine enemies, and an adversary unto thine adversaries.
Exodus 23:22 (KJV)

Therefore all they that devour thee shall be devoured; and all thine adversaries, every one of them, shall go into captivity; and they that spoil thee shall be a spoil, and all that prey upon thee will I give for a prey.
Jeremiah 30:16 (KJV)

34.  Release the fire of God against everything that has made itself your adversary

35.  Declare boldly that according to God's Word every enemy of your peace shall be broken to pieces

36.  Pray that the Lord would arise and break in pieces every instrument of the oppressor

37.  Declare frustration for every weapon of the wicked

38.  Decree that all that lift up themselves against you shall be cut off - Micah 5:9

> Thine hand shall be lifted up upon thine adversaries,
> and all thine enemies shall be cut off.
> Micah 5:9 (KJV)

39.  Rejoice because the Mighty Terrible One is with you

40.  Decree that the weapons of the enemy shall not prosper but rather they would receive embarrassment and shame

41.  No matter what their might is, declare that every enemy who rises against you shall be smitten before your face

42.    Thank God for the victories of the past and give Him praise for the one He will achieve today in your life - Joshua 1:5

There shall not any man be able to stand before thee all the days of thy life: as I was with Moses, so I will be with thee: I will not fail thee, nor forsake thee.
Joshua 1:5 (KJV)

43.    Bring the fire of God against every instrument of the enemy; scorpions, serpents and whatever they sent against your peace

44.    Declare and decree that the Lord fights against those who fight against you

45.    Go into the realm of the spirit and cut every tongue and silence every word contrary to your promotion

46.    Boldly declare that every evil decision contrary to your destiny, counsel and purpose shall not stand because God is with you - Isaiah 8:10

Take counsel together, and it shall come to nought; speak the word, and it shall not stand: for God is with us.
Isaiah 8:10 (KJV)

47.    Declare that with your eyes only would you see the reward of the wicked

48. Take authority over every form of oppression and declare that in its place you shall be established in righteousness

49. Bring the fire of God against every force that is opposing your progress

50. I send the fire of God to the camp of every demon entity assigned to fight me

51. Every satanic resistance shall not stand in the name of the Lord

52. I call upon the Lord this day and decree my deliverance from every trouble

53. Every contract of evil signed by the enemy for my harm shall meet with failure

54. Pray that the plan of every evil neighbour will be put to shame

55. Receive the grace of God for vigilance and alertness in Jesus name

56. Declare and decree that the verbal destruction of Sanballat and Tobias will turn around to become a blessing

57. Every unholy gathering that is contrary to the purpose of God will be scattered by the Holy Ghost

58.    Receive the grace to be watchful day and night and not to be loose in the things of the Spirit - Nehemiah 4:9

Nevertheless we made our prayer unto our God, and set a watch against them day and night, because of them.
Nehemiah 4:9 (KJV)

59.    Receive the grace and power to be watchful against attack of the enemy - Nehemiah 4:13

Therefore set I in the lower places behind the wall, and on the higher places, I even set the people after their families with their swords, their spears, and their bows.
Nehemiah 4:13 (KJV)

60.    Receive divine intervention for every situation you are confronted with in Jesus name

61.    Pray that every trap the enemy is setting will be exposed to you

62.    Cast down every stronghold of the enemy that is trying to hold you in an old pattern of failure

63.    God who has given me vision would also make it happen in Jesus name - Isaiah 66:9

Shall I bring to the birth, and not cause to bring forth? saith the LORD: shall I cause to bring forth, and shut

the womb? saith thy God.
Isaiah 66:9 (KJV)

64. Every lying spirit militating against my purpose and assignment would receive the fire of God

65. I declare that my fear and dread shall fill the enemy's heart

66. The expectation of the envious concerning me will meet with frustration

67. Declare and decree that every plan of the enemy will meet with frustration - Job 5:12

68. Pray that those who are putting you down out of jealousy will be disgraced and put to shame

69. I decree my prosperity in the midst of hostility

70. Declare that this is the year the enemies of your progress will be put to shame

71. Declare that every attempt of the enemy to make you miss your destined grace, blessing and purpose will meet with frustration

72. Command the treasures of the sea to begin to come into your hand

73.    Command the treasures of the sand to begin to come into your hand

74.    Pray that whatever has stopped you from entering into your Wealthy Place will experience a turnaround - 2 Corinthians 3:16

> Nevertheless when it shall turn to the Lord, the vail shall be taken away.
> 2 Corinthians 3:16 (KJV)

75.    Declare  boldly that you refuse to bow to every terror of the enemy

76.    Declare that according to God's Word you shall be far from terror

77.    Command every wicked spirit to come out of their hiding place in any aspect of your life

# THE SPIRIT OF SORCERY

1.      Declare your freedom in the name of the Lord

2.      Give God militant praise as a sign that the devil's time is over in your life - Revelation 12:12

Therefore rejoice, ye heavens, and ye that dwell in them. Woe to the inhabiters of the earth and of the sea! for the devil is come down unto you, having great wrath, because he knoweth that he hath but a short time.
Revelation 12:12 (KJV)

3.      Take back your glorious future which has been stolen by the Jezebels of this world

4.      Declare   that God will destroy every ungodly imagination intended for your hurt

5.      Ask the Lord to open your eyes to see every evil plan of the enemy being cooked up in secret places

6.      Declare that those who say that it is over their dead body that you would receive breakthrough, that their prophesy will come to pass - Exodus 10:29

7.      Renounce your  covenant with every ungodly spirit; Beelzebub, Jezebel, Ancestral spirits in the name of Jesus

8.      Destroy every peg used to fasten you down, limiting your movement in life in the name of the Lord - Isaiah 22:25

In that day, saith the LORD of hosts, shall the nail that is fastened in the sure place be removed, and be cut down, and fall; and the burden that was upon it shall be cut off: for the LORD hath spoken it.
Isaiah 22:25 (KJV)

9.      Declare your freedom from every satanic containment

10.    I reject every demonic, satanic, life-limiting name that may have been given or called - 1 Chronicles 4:9-10

And Jabez was more honourable than his brethren: and his mother called his name Jabez, saying, Because I bare him with sorrow. And Jabez called on the God of Israel, saying, Oh that thou wouldest bless me indeed, and enlarge my coast, and that thine hand might be with me, and that thou wouldest keep me from evil, that it may not grieve me! And God granted him that which he requested.
1 Chronicles 4:9-10 (KJV)

11.    Every witch and bloodsucker will suck their own blood

12.    Every unclean spirit that have ruled over your family and community will have no control over your life from now on in the name of the Lord

13.    Thank the Lord because no evil intended to be used against you will be found - Daniel 6:4-5

Then the presidents and princes sought to find occasion against Daniel concerning the kingdom; but they could find none occasion nor fault; forasmuch as he was faithful, neither was there any error or fault found in him. Then said these men, We shall not find any occasion against this Daniel, except we find it against him concerning the law of his God.
Daniel 6:4-5 (KJV)

14. Declare boldly that every satanic embargo hindering what belongs to you is removed right now in the name of the Lord

15. Pray that those who are seeking to edge you out of your blessing will themselves be embarrassed and be put to shame

16. Decree that those who are trying to belittle you will 'be little'

17. Declare that every satanic enchantment put together against you shall not work

18. Rebuke the source of every witchcraft and divination intended for your downfall

19. Declare that according to God's Word a plague shall come upon them that express hatred against you

20. Boldly declare that though you have fallen you will rise again - Judges 16:22

Howbeit the hair of his head began to grow again after he was shaven.
Judges 16:22 (KJV)

21. Every strange relation who is praying for my right to be held back, the Lord will expose them

22.    Command frustration on those assigned by the enemy to "touch your inheritance"

23.    Command the fire of God against those who are working aggressively against your blessing - Jeremiah 12:14-15

And he had forty sons and thirty nephews, that rode on threescore and ten ass colts: and he judged Israel eight years. And Abdon the son of Hillel the Pirathonite died, and was buried in Pirathon in the land of Ephraim, in the mount of the Amalekites.
Judges 12:14-15 (KJV)

24.    Reject and refuse every defamatory name they have given to you to put you down

25.    Receive divine acceleration rather to fulfil the call of God upon your life

26.    Receive the success that will bring embarrassment on those who will put you down

27.    Break the spell of every form of bewitching that you may have fallen under

28.    Break the spell of witchcraft that may have held the people around you

29.    Take authority over the city, and the locality where you live and destroy the spell of witchcraft which holds

the area - Acts 8:9-11

> But there was a certain man, called Simon, which
> beforetime in the same city used sorcery, and bewitched
> the people of Samaria, giving out that himself was
> some great one: To whom they all gave heed, from the
> least to the greatest, saying, This man is the great power
> of God. And to him they had regard, because that of
> long time he had bewitched them with sorceries.
> Acts 8:9-11 (KJV)

30.    Command every contrary spirit that is trying to
hold you down to leave and get out in the name of the
Lord - Acts 16:16-18

> And it came to pass, as we went to prayer, a certain
> damsel possessed with a spirit of divination met us,
> which brought her masters much gain by soothsaying:
> The same followed Paul and us, and cried, saying,
> These men are the servants of the most high God,
> which shew unto us the way of salvation. And this did
> she many days. But Paul, being grieved, turned and said
> to the spirit, I command thee in the name of Jesus
> Christ to come out of her. And he came out the same
> hour.
> Acts 16:16-18 (KJV)

31.    Receive God's divine intervention in every
situation where the enemy is trying to attack you through
witchcraft

32.     Nullify every statement of witchcraft made out of jealousy against you

33.     Declare that the counsel of evil people will have no effect - Psalms 33:10

The LORD bringeth the counsel of the heathen to nought: he maketh the devices of the people of none effect.
Psalms 33:10 (KJV)

34.     Declare and decree that you refuse to permit anything that wants to limit the calling and greatness God has destined for your life

35.     Declare every gate of limitation resistance and hindrance which the enemy has erected to be null and void in Jesus name

36.     Cast down every demonic gate of the mind that tries to belittle and stop you from the favour of God

37.     I boldly declare He who began a good work in me will perfect it

38.     Decree that every plan of the enemy to make you lose your mind will meet with frustration in the name of the Lord - 1 Samuel 16:14: 18:10

39.     Thank God because the day has come for every shadow satan has cast over your joy, over your blessing,

over your work to begin to move away

40.     Declare and decree that every satanic covering intended to veil your beauty and glory will be torn apart in the name of the Lord

41.     Pray that the power that tore the veil of the temple would tear every satanic tarpaulin covering the glory of God in your life - Isaiah 25:7-8

And he will destroy in this mountain the face of the covering cast over all people, and the vail that is spread over all nations.  He will swallow up death in victory; and the Lord GOD will wipe away tears from off all faces; and the rebuke of his people shall he take away from off all the earth: for the LORD hath spoken it.
Isaiah 25:7-8 (KJV)

42.     Boldly proclaim that every satanic "purdah" thrown over your face to hide the grace of God is torn by the Holy Ghost

43.     Every move by ungodly superiors to put you in the place where you shall be forgotten will be frustrated by God

44.     Every satanic veil intended to cover you and make you forgotten will be torn by God

45. Declare by faith that those who are waiting to see what will happen to you, will see the glory of God

46. Pull down every covering placed upon your life, intended to limit your level of operation

47. Pull down every covering placed upon your life intended to limit the blessing of your life

48. Break free from every satanic oppression - Acts 10:38

How God anointed Jesus of Nazareth with the Holy Ghost and with power: who went about doing good, and healing all that were oppressed of the devil; for God was with him.
Acts 10:38 (KJV)

# THE SPIRIT OF REBELLION

1.    Boldly declare that everyone who has made himself a channel of offence be put to shame - Matthew 18:7

> Woe unto the world because of offences! for it must needs be that offences come; but woe to that man by whom the offense cometh!
> Matthew 18:7 (KJV)

2.    Prophesy that every rebel in your dwelling place, office or sphere of operation will dwell in dry places - Psalms 68:6

God setteth the solitary in families: he bringeth out those which are bound with chains: but the rebellious dwell in a dry land.
Psalms 68:6 (KJV)

3.      The Lord will release His hornets to chase every evil gathering - Exodus23:28

And I will send hornets before thee, which shall drive out the Hivite, the Canaanite, and the Hittite, from before thee.
Exodus 23:28 (KJV)

4.      Declare that the Lord will be an enemy to those who have made themselves your enemy - Exodus 23:22

But if thou shalt indeed obey his voice, and do all that I speak; then I will be an enemy unto thine enemies, and an adversary unto thine adversaries.
Exodus 23:22 (KJV)

5.      Just as the earth opened its mouth and swallowed the agents of wickedness - every contrary force shall come to nothing - Numbers 16:32

And the earth opened her mouth, and swallowed them up, and their houses, and all the men that appertained unto Korah, and all their goods.
Numbers 16:32 (KJV)

6.      Release God's consuming fire against every

gathering of wickedness

7. Pray that the conspiracy of conspirators will work against them

8. Boldly declare that those who do not refrain their tongue will suffer the consequence

9. Pray that every evil that has been spoken against you where you work or do your business will be exposed by the Lord

10. Come against every satanic principality where you live and declare that their effort against you shall not stand

11. Declare boldly that the enemies of God who are also your enemy shall bow by reason of His goodness - Psalms 66:3

Say unto God, How terrible art thou in thy works! through the greatness of thy power shall thine enemies submit themselves unto thee.
Psalms 66:3 (KJV)

12. Declare that the seat will be too hot for those who are sitting illegally on your property

13. Pray that those who are sitting and planning an illegal transfer for you from your place of planting will be put to shame

14.    Pray that every rebel and pretender hanging around you will be exposed by the Lord

15.    Receive the grace of God against every Korah spirit that has risen in insolence against you

16.    Pray that your eyes will be open to know and to move away
from everyone with a Korah spirit - Numbers 16:23-24

And the LORD spake unto Moses, saying,  Speak unto the congregation, saying, Get you up from about the tabernacle of Korah, Dathan, and Abiram.
Numbers 16:23-24 (KJV)

17.    Decree that every voice that is grumbling against you, that have risen in gossip and virulence will be silenced by the Lord

18.    Everyone raised by satan to plan fleshly, satanic vendetta against you will suffer the consequence

19.    Pray that the  folly of everyone with a Korah spirit will become apparent to all men - 2 Timothy 3:8-9

Now as Jannes and Jambres withstood Moses, so do these also resist the truth: men of corrupt minds, reprobate concerning the faith.  But they shall proceed no further: for their folly shall be manifest unto all men, as theirs also was.
2 Timothy 3:8-9 (KJV)

20.    Decree that the ungodly schemes of every Korah around you will fail and their pride will drive them out

21.    Pray that those who are watching you, seeking to accuse you, will be embarrassed and put to shame

22.    Decree the justice of God against every form of wickedness from here to the ends of the earth

23.    Release confusion into the camp of the enemy - Jeremiah 20:11

24.    Pray that those who have come against you ganging up shall all scatter in seven ways - Deuteronomy 28:7

> The LORD shall cause thine enemies that rise up against thee to be smitten before thy face: they shall come out against thee one way, and flee before thee seven ways.
> Deuteronomy 28:7 (KJV)

25.    Proclaim boldly that all those who lift themselves in arrogance shall be humbled before you

26.    Pray that the ganging up of the enemy will result in them tearing one another apart - Isaiah 49:25-26

> But thus saith the LORD, Even the captives of the mighty shall be taken away, and the prey of the terrible shall be delivered: for I will contend with him that contendeth with thee, and I will save thy children. And I will feed them that oppress thee with their own flesh;

and they shall be drunken with their own blood, as with sweet wine: and all flesh shall know that I the LORD am thy Saviour and thy Redeemer, the mighty One of Jacob.
Isaiah 49:25-26 (KJV)

27.     Declare and decree that those who take counsel together against you shall end up in embarrassment

28.     Prophesy that every ganging up of wickedness shall end up in their shame

29.     Pray that frustration will be the result of every evil board meeting intended against you

30.     Declare that every evil gathering intended to be against you shall result in falling apart - Isaiah 54:14-15

In righteousness shalt thou be established: thou shalt be far from oppression; for thou shalt not fear: and from terror; for it shall not come near thee.  Behold, they  shall surely gather together, but not by me: whosoever shall gather together against thee shall fall for thy sake.
Isaiah 54:14-15 (KJV)

31.     Ask  the Lord to expose all the foolishness that has been plotted against you - 2 Timothy 3:9

But they shall proceed no further: for their folly shall be manifest unto all men, as theirs also was.
2 Timothy 3:9 (KJV)

32.    Decree that the voice of the critics shall be silenced in the name of the Lord

33.    I boldly declare that I scale over every wicked plot to distract me from accomplishing my goals - God will put to shame all those who have ganged up to fight His work in my life

34.    Declare and decree that the conspiracy of all conspirators will work against them - Nehemiah 6:1-4

Now it came to pass, when Sanballat, and Tobiah, and Geshem the Arabian, and the rest of our enemies, heard that I had builded the wall, and that there was no breach left therein; (though at that time I had not set up the doors upon the gates;) That Sanballat and Geshem sent unto me, saying, Come, let us meet together in some one of the villages in the plain of Ono. But they thought to do me mischief. And I sent messengers unto them, saying, I am doing a great work, so that I cannot come down: why should the work cease, whilst I leave it, and come down to you? Yet they sent unto me four times after this sort; and I answered them after the same manner.
Nehemiah 6:1-4 (KJV)

35.    Receive boldness and strength that will belittle mockery, slander and opposition in your life

36.    Pray that the evil and the iniquity of those who are plotting against you will be exposed for everyone to see

37.     Release the anger and fire of God against plotters of evil who have risen against you - Nehemiah 4:4-5

Hear, O our God; for we are despised: and turn their reproach upon their own head, and give them for a prey in the land of captivity:
Nehemiah 4:4 (KJV)

38.     Pray that God will expose every merchant of evil who is plotting against you

39.     Thank God because the evil counsel of wicked men will meet with the frustration of God

40.     Those who are planning for my downfall and raising barriers will themselves fall into their own trap

41.     Every evil man or woman who have a man to quench my start, their plans will meet with frustration

42.     Reject and refuse every tendency of rebellion against those who have leadership over you

43.     Reject and refuse the branding and the name "trouble maker"

44.     Ask the Lord to set you free from every carnality that makes you want to rise against those above you

45.     Pray that the spirit of Absalom that is frustrating the local church where you belong will be frustrated by the Lord

46.    Free yourself from a religious spirit that puts down the leaders over you

47.    Receive God's grace and humility for every situation

48.    Repent of every Saulish spirit of pride and empty religion

49.    Repent of every tendency to depend on your human strength - 1 Samuel 2:9

He will keep the feet of his saints, and the wicked shall be silent in darkness; for by strength shall no man prevail.
1 Samuel 2:9 (KJV)

# THE SPIRIT OF BLOCKAGE & BARRIERS

1.     Declare that wickedness shall fizzle at your gate because you follow the counsel of the Lord - Proverbs 14:19

> The evil bow before the good; and the wicked at the gates of the righteous.
> Proverbs 14:19 (KJV)

2.     Every stone rolled out against you shall hit the sender

3.    Release the fire wall of God around yourself, your family and all that belongs to you

4.    Declare that every spirit intruding into your destiny shall be blinded by the Lord - Genesis 19:11

And they smote the men that were at the door of the house with blindness, both small and great: so that they wearied themselves to find the door.
Genesis 19:11 (KJV)

5.    Boldly declare that all those who rise in oppression against you will eat their own flesh

6.    Declare yourself free from every form of collective captivity your community leaders have covenanted you into

7.    Thank the Lord because He will frustrate the token of liars and the evil speeches of those who want to destroy you

8.    Pray that the Lord will expose the evil intention of those who are attacking you verbally

9.    Come against the spirit that is hindering the manifestation of what God has already done for you

10.    Decree that the rod of the wicked in every form shall be destroyed - Psalms 125:3

For the rod of the wicked shall not rest upon the lot of
the righteous; lest the righteous put forth their hands
unto iniquity.
Psalms 125:3 (KJV)

11.    Release ministering angels to begin to intercept
and pull in favours that belongs to you

12.    Decree that God will use every instrument of war
to destroy their hindrance in your life

13.    Eject every squatter occupying houses that
rightfully belong to you in the realm of the spirit

14.    Pray that your eyes will be open to know and
expose the real enemy of your soul

15.    Declare that those who are imposing themselves
on you will find their way slippery in the name of the
Lord

16.    Boldly declare that those who have gone too far in
their attack of your life and commitment to God be put
to shame

17.    I boldly declare that I am too heavy for the devil
to carry

18.    Bless the Lord because He will lift up your hand
against the enemy

19.   I boldly proclaim that I will complete my assignment and satan's hindrances be frustrated

20.   I reject and release myself from every ungodly appetite meant for bondage

21.   Ask the Lord to open your eye to know every strange relation, neighbour and friend around you

22.   Ask the Lord for wisdom to bridle your tongue and not expose the secrets of life - Proverbs 29:11

> A fool uttereth all his mind: but a wise man keepeth it
> in till afterwards.
> Proverbs 29:11 (KJV)

23.   Those who are creating impossibilities and barriers in your way shall themselves never see possibilities

24.   Those who have made themselves agents of hindrance shall be put to shame - Nehemiah 4:8

> And conspired all of them together to come and to
> fight against Jerusalem, and to hinder it.
> Nehemiah 4:8 (KJV)

25.   Neutralise by the power of the Holy Ghost every thing sent against your life including anger, mockery and the temptation to compromise

26.     Pray that those who are causing a distraction and hindering your promotion will move in Jesus Name

27.     Ask the Lord to expose every unclean spirit that wants to jump suddenly on you - Nehemiah 4:9

Nevertheless we made our prayer unto our God, and set a watch against them day and night, because of them.
Nehemiah 4:9 (KJV)

28.     Prophesy that your "see nothing days" will begin to change to the days of abundance

29.     Repent of every disobedience that has blocked the blessings of God

30.     Release God's fire against every limitation and barrier which satan is putting before you

31.     Boldly prophesy that no weapon of satan will stop you from maximising your potential

32.     Pray that in every area of your life you will break barriers and maximise your potential

33.     Declare that every gate, every obstacle, barrier or barricade between you and your destiny shall be frustrated by the Lord

34.     Receive boldness from the Lord to rise and smash every obstacle of satan

35.    Receive divine access into what God has destined for your inheritance

36.    Boldly proclaim that every demonic gate of brass is torn down

37.    All the iron bars which the enemy has put in place to try to stop you from reaching where you are going will not work in Jesus name

38.    Every human barrier which satan has ordained to thwart your vision, will themselves be moved away by God

39.    Bring the fire of God against every demonic gate erected to disturb or limit your flow

40.    Receive the mantle of a barrier breaker and pass through all the gates the enemy said you would never pass - Micah 2:3; Psalms 24:7-9

Therefore thus saith the LORD; Behold, against this family do I devise an evil, from which ye shall not remove your necks; neither shall ye go haughtily: for this time is evil.
Micah 2:3 (KJV)

Lift up your heads, O ye gates; and be ye lift up, ye everlasting doors; and the King of glory shall come in. Who is this King of glory? The LORD strong and

mighty, the LORD mighty in battle.
Lift up your heads, O ye gates; even lift them up, ye
everlasting doors; and the King of glory shall come in.
Psalms 24:7-9 (KJV)

41.    Command doors that have been shut for a long time to begin to open up to you

42.    Declare  that in spite of the negatives you are hearing and seeing, your life is going forward

43.    Reject and refuse every spirit that is working and producing inaccessibilities

44.    Command  every door before you that has demonic padlocks to begin to break open in the name of Jesus

45.    Receive the grace to break out from obscurity to favour; from isolation to complete participation in what will result in your promotion

46.    Bring the fire of God against any veil that is blocking you from fruitfulness

47.    Ask  the  Lord  to  remove everything that is blocking your way to greatness

48.    Pray that you will begin to discover every hidden treasure that was meant for you

49.   Uproot and destroy the root of every ungodly spirit that is tormenting your life

# THE SPIRIT OF DISCOURAGEMENT

1.    Boldly proclaim that all evil shall bow before the goodness of the Lord in your life

2.    Boldly declare that like Haman's counsel against Mordecai; every evil counsel against you will turn around for your promotion

3.    Declare boldly that the revolving door of failure, retardation and loss is permanently shut in Jesus name

4.    Thank the Lord because He will cause your excellence and diligence to speak for you

5.    Pray that all those who are waiting to blackmail you will be exposed by the Lord

6.    Pray boldly that the mouth of every evil speaker will be stopped - Psalms 63:11

> But the king shall rejoice in God; every one that
> sweareth by him shall glory: but the mouth of them
> that speak lies shall be stopped.
> Psalms 63:11 (KJV)

7.    Thank God because He will silence the Sanballats who are opposers of good things in your life

8.    Decree and declare that the expectation of the ungodly concerning you will be frustrated

9.    Reject every satanic lie that is tempting you to move away from where God has ordained for your blessing - Genesis 26:12,13

> Then Isaac sowed in that land, and received in the
> same year an hundredfold: and the LORD blessed him.
> And the man waxed great, and went forward, and grew
> until he became very great:
> Genesis 26:12-13 (KJV)

10.    Thank God that because you abide and trust in Him, you will not be moved - Psalms 125:1

They that trust in the LORD shall be as mount Zion,
which cannot be removed, but abideth for ever.
Psalms 125:1 (KJV)

11 But the king shall rejoice in God; every one that
sweareth by him shall glory: but the mouth of them that
speak lies shall be stopped.
Psalms 63:11 (KJV)

But the king shall rejoice in God; every one that
sweareth by him shall glory: but the mouth of them
that speak lies shall be stopped.
Psalms 63:11 (KJV)

11.   Release  the fire of God against every satanic
activity trying to make you depart from the faith

12.   Give  God  praise because in the middle of the
battle God will lift your horn of anointing - 1 Samuel
2:10

The adversaries of the LORD shall be broken to
pieces; out of heaven shall he thunder upon them: the
LORD shall judge the ends of the earth; and he shall
give strength unto his king, and exalt the horn of his
anointed.
1 Samuel 2:10 (KJV)

13.   Thank God because He shall procure justice for
you as His people - Psalms 72:4

He shall judge the poor of the people, he shall save the

children of the needy, and shall break in pieces the
oppressor.
Psalms 72:4 (KJV)

14. Pray that the wicked and the persecutors shall
stumble

15. Declare that in spite of their attack and effort they
will not prevail

16. Pray that the wicked shall not be able to proceed
further with their intention

17. Every act of wickedness planned against me shall
meet with frustration

18. Decree that the provocation of your adversaries
would only result in your promotion

19. Declare and decree that out of the satanic attack
and provocation God will bring forth a breakthrough for
you

20. Declare and decree that every instrument of
ridicule will end up producing a miracle

21. Those who are belittling the great work of God
declare that they shall be put to shame

22. Receive the success that will end up being mental

punishment for your enemies in Jesus

23.    Thank God because you will turn the reproach and the spite of your adversaries to your testimony - Nehemiah 4:4-5

Hear, O our God; for we are despised: and turn their reproach upon their own head, and give them for a prey in the land of captivity: And cover not their iniquity, and let not their sin be blotted out from before thee: for they have provoked thee to anger before the builders.
Nehemiah 4:4-5 (KJV)

24.    Pray for the grace to be watchful and not to take anything for granted

25.    Pray for a divine turnaround in every business endeavour

26.    Confess that your tears and fears shall turn around to jubilation

27.    Pray that your eyes will be open to discover the unusual miracles waiting for you where you have known frustration

28.    I come against every spirit behind destructive experiences in my life

29.    Receive divine cleansing from your mind from

every negative meditation

30.    Every trash satan is piling up and trying to pour into your heart, declare that you are not a collector of trash and it does not belong in your heart in the name of the Lord

31.    Bind the spirit that is restless and never stays in one place and command it to leave

32.    Receive    deliverance    from    the    spirit    of discouragement

33.    In the face of every delay receive the grace to declare that God's strength is your joy - Isaiah 61:3; Nehemiah 8:10

To appoint unto them that mourn in Zion, to give unto them beauty for ashes, the oil of joy for mourning, the garment of praise for the spirit of heaviness; that they might be called trees of righteousness, the planting of the LORD, that he might be glorified.
Isaiah 61:3 (KJV)

Then he said unto them, Go your way, eat the fat, and drink the sweet, and send portions unto them for whom nothing is prepared: for this day is holy unto our Lord: neither be ye sorry; for the joy of the LORD is your strength.
Nehemiah 8:10 (KJV)

34. Receive the grace to act contrary to satan's expectation in the midst of your battles and troubles

35. Declare that in spite of the discouragement you see, you will hope in God - Romans 4:17-18

(As it is written, I have made thee a father of many nations,) before him whom he believed, even God, who quickeneth the dead, and calleth those things which be not as though they were.
Who against hope believed in hope, that he might become the father of many nations, according to that which was spoken, So shall thy seed be.
Romans 4:17-18 (KJV)

36. Receive the grace to take bold steps in the midst of discouragement

37. Declare to every false lying spirit that in spite of what you see, the Lord is the strength of your life

38. Receive grace to focus on the greatness of God and not the magnitude of the problem

39. Prophesy life where there is an appearance of an apparent death - 1 Kings 19:4

But he himself went a day's journey into the wilderness, and came and sat down under a juniper tree: and he requested for himself that he might die; and

said, It is enough; now, O LORD, take away my life; for
I am not better than my fathers.

1 Kings 19:4 (KJV)

40.    Send the fire of God against every barrier
of discouragement    and declare that you are
unstoppable

# THE SPIRIT OF SORCERY & WITCHCRAFT

1.  Boldly declare that the instrument of every transmitter of evil shall be destroyed

2.  The counsel of every invisible wickedness shall be frustrated in the Name of Jesus - Psalms 91:14-16

Because he hath set his love upon me, therefore will I deliver him: I will set him on high, because he hath known my name. He shall call upon me, and I will

answer him: I will be with him in trouble; I will deliver
him, and honour him. With long life will I satisfy him,
and shew him my salvation.
Psalms 91:14-16 (KJV)

3.     Thank God because the magicians of Egypt will
not be able to stand the grace of God upon your life -
Exodus 9:11

And the magicians could not stand before Moses
because of the boils; for the boil was upon the
magicians, and upon all the Egyptians.
Exodus 9:11 (KJV)

4.     Decree that every evil enchantment spoken
against you will not stand in the name of the Lord

5.     Release the fire of God against every diviner
and their divination - Numbers 23:23

Surely there is no enchantment against Jacob, neither is
there any divination against Israel: according to this
time it shall be said of Jacob and of Israel, What hath
God wrought!
Numbers 23:23 (KJV)

6.     Proclaim boldly that every scourge of premature
death will pass over you and your children

7.     Release the grace that will cause men to act

contrary to how they planned and release the blessing which belongs to you which they are standing on

8.    Curse every seducing spirit that is trying to draw you away from the counsel of God for your life

9.    Bring the blood of Jesus against every pathological jealousy that has risen against you

10.    Contrary to the plan of the enemy prophesy in advance that the world will see what God would do in your life - Numbers 23:23

Surely there is no enchantment against Jacob, neither is there any divination against Israel: according to this time it shall be said of Jacob and of Israel, What hath God wrought!
Numbers 23:23 (KJV)

11.    Declare that God will not hearken to the voice of every Baalam that is cursing what belongs to you

12.    Prophesy that every curse pronounced against your blessing, your work, your property will turn around for blessing

13.    I plead the blood of Jesus against every plague, every pestilence which the enemy is perpetrating

14.    I boldly declare my life is sealed with the Holy Ghost

15.    My life is a no go area to every demonic entity

16.    Declare and decree that every curse, every negative spoken against your work, your vision and your life will be cancelled by God's glory

17.    Every evil prophecy that is brought against your vision and calling declare that it shall not stand

18.    Pray that every tongue that brings a slander against your peace and joy will be silenced in the name of the Lord - Nehemiah 6:5-9

Then sent Sanballat his servant unto me in like manner
the fifth time with an open letter in his hand;
Wherein was written, It is reported among the heathen,
and Gashmu saith it, that thou and the Jews think to
rebel: for which cause thou buildest the wall, that thou
mayest be their king, according to these words.
And thou hast also appointed prophets to preach of
thee at Jerusalem, saying, There is a king in Judah: and
now shall it be reported to the king according to these
words. Come now therefore, and let us take counsel
together.   Then I sent unto him, saying, There are no
such things done as thou sayest, but thou feignest them
out of thine own heart.  For they all made us afraid,
saying, Their hands shall be weakened from the work,
that it be not done. Now therefore, O God, strengthen
my hands.
Nehemiah 6:5-9 (KJV)

19.   Pray that everybody who is sent to frustrate your prophetic assignment will be exposed

20.   Declare  and decree that every false prophecy spoken to deter you will be negated by the Holy Ghost

21.   Declare and decree that the spirit of Baalam called to curse your work will be frustrated

22.   Release the fire of God against every satanic enchantment put together against you - Numbers 23:23

Surely there is no enchantment against Jacob, neither is there any divination against Israel: according to this time it shall be said of Jacob and of Israel, What hath God wrought!
Numbers 23:23 (KJV)

23.   Rebuke every  Satanistic spirit behind sorcery, divination, and witchcraft that is being used against you

24.   Boldly declare that no divination, no hex, put together against you will stand

25.   Revoke every curse that is placed on you known or unknown in the name of Jesus

26.   Send the fire of God to scatter all those people who are evoking every word of divination, enchantment and sorcery against you

27.   Declare null and void every pronouncement that is made against you as a curse

28.   Declare boldly that no curse of your adversaries would alight

29.   Decree and declare that their sorcery would have no power over you

30.   Boldly proclaim that you are for signs and wonders, not for curses and witchcraft attacks

31.   Prophesy against all lovers of money who are cursing you in private because they are inadequately paid

32.   Thank the Lord because every curse pronounced against you results in your promotion and blessing because of the love of God

33.   Boldly declare that in spite of people's pronouncements only the counsel of God will be established - Proverbs 19:21

There are many devices in a man's heart; nevertheless the counsel of the LORD, that shall stand.
Proverbs 19:21 (KJV)

34.   Pray that the Lord will expose to you the secret behind all those doing magical signs and wonders that are not of God

35.     Cancel every demonic decree that has been made against your peace

36.     Nullify every evil pronouncement from the pit of hell

37.     Declare null and void every curse and every spell that has been placed upon your life

38.     Bring the blood of Jesus against every satanic curse

39.     Declare and decree that every statement contrary to the purpose of God for your life will not stand and is therefore renounced

40.     Bring yourself  under the cleansing of the blood of Jesus from family, national and generational curses

41.     Boldly declare that the spell is broken over your life to the third and fourth generation

42.     Cancel every vow, every decision, every statement you have made that has justified satanic veils in your life

43.     Destroy every inner vow that has produced a veil and is hindering you from receiving marital proposals

44.     Every seed and plant in your life, work or business which God has not planted must be uprooted in Jesus

name - Matthew 15:13

But he answered and said, Every plant, which my
heavenly Father hath not planted, shall be rooted up.
Matthew 15:13 (KJV)

45.    Release the fire of God to burn to the root
whatever God did not initiate in your life

46.    Pray that the fire that purified Isaiah's mouth will
bring purification to your destiny - Isaiah 6:7

And he laid it upon my mouth, and said, Lo, this hath
touched thy lips; and thine iniquity is taken away, and
thy sin purged.
Isaiah 6:7 (KJV)

47.    Declare that because the Lord is with you, no evil
seed of satan will bring forth fruit

# THE SPIRIT OF PARALYSIS

1.    Declare that the wickedness of the wicked will come to an end in your life

2.    Declare that everything that has made you impotent: spiritually, financially, physically is broken from today in Jesus Name

3.    Declare  by faith that you receive the power to produce and reproduce - 2 Kings 9:32

And he lifted up his face to the window, and said, Who is on my side? who? And there looked out to him two

or three eunuchs.
2 Kings 9:32 (KJV)

4.      Boldly declare that you incubate the future and you shall give birth to a great destiny

5.      Boldly declare that the stones with which you were fired shall return to those who shot it - Proverbs 26:27

> Whoso diggeth a pit shall fall therein: and he that rolleth a stone, it will return upon him.
> Proverbs 26:27 (KJV)

6.      Thank God because every demonic Herod seeking your life will be silenced by the Holy Spirit

7.      Boldly call back all stolen items and properties in the name of Jesus

8.      Take authority over every satanic weapon and declare that God's power will swallow up the weapons of the enemy - Exodus 7:12

> For they cast down every man his rod, and they became serpents: but Aaron's rod swallowed up their rods.
> Exodus 7:12 (KJV)

9.      Pray that the finger of God will be manifested against every satanic attack - Exodus 8:19

Then the magicians said unto Pharaoh, This is the
finger of God: and Pharaoh's heart was hardened, and
he hearkened not unto them; as the LORD had said.
Exodus 8:19 (KJV)

10.   Command all doors of entrance for demons be
shut up for ever in the name of the Lord

11.   I cancel every evil pronouncement made into my
life from childhood

12.   All those who sit down and devise mischief
against my life shall be put to shame

13.   Boldly declare that all those who rise in
oppression against you will eat their own flesh

14.   Declare yourself free from every form of collective
captivity your family elders have brought you into in the
name of the Lord

15.   Loose yourself from the grip of the spirit of
infirmity - Luke 13:12

And when Jesus saw her, he called her to him, and said
unto her, Woman, thou art loosed from thine infirmity.
Luke 13:12 (KJV)

16.   Take authority over every spirit of wickedness and
wicked forces that are at work right now in your life and
break their grip

17.    Boldly declare that the weapon of delay and lack shall no longer work in your life in the name of Jesus

18.    Lift up your voice in praise to God because your hope shall not be in vain

19.    Bring the blood of Jesus against the spirit that wants you to behold good things but not taste it

20.    Boldly declare that you have been given all things richly to enjoy

21.    Boldly declare that there shall be a performance of what God has spoken into your life -    Ezekiel 12:25

For I am the LORD: I will speak, and the word that I shall speak shall come to pass; it shall be no more prolonged: for in your days, O rebellious house, will I say the word, and will perform it, saith the Lord GOD. Ezekiel 12:25 (KJV)

22.    Declare that the power that rose Jesus from the dead   will   bring back to life every dead area of your blessing

23.    Reject the scourge of lack and declare God's abundance in your life

24.    Come against the spirit that wants to make you plant and not eat the fruit of your labour

25.    Decree and declare that where they expected your downfall, God will turn it around for your promotion

26.    Release the fire of God against every demonic activity intended to blindfold you from your blessing

27.    Release the fire of God against all demonic activity trying to affect your vision

28.    Ask the Lord to expose every desert place which the enemy has planned for you

29.    Pray that every weapon of satan intended to rip you apart and defame you will be brought to shame

30.    Pray that every weapon of satan intended to rip you apart and defame you will be brought to shame

31.    Declare that according to God's Word those that are devouring you will be devoured themselves

32.    Whatever has set itself up to spoil you shall be spoiled

33.    Every situation that wants to turn you to a prey shall itself become a prey in the name of the Lord

34.    Decree death to the life supply of wickedness

35.    Pray that the arm the wicked stretched out to do evil, will be destroyed - Psalms 37:17

For the arms of the wicked shall be broken: but the
LORD upholdeth the righteous.
Psalms 37:17 (KJV)

36.     Declare that in spite of the attack of the enemy,
the mighty arm of God will uphold you - Psalms 37:17

For the arms of the wicked shall be broken: but the
LORD upholdeth the righteous.
Psalms 37:17 (KJV)

37.     Rejoice in advance that the Lord will not fail you
or forsake you

38.     Give God praise because He will not fail your nor
forsake you

39.     Pray that in spite of their attacks the Lord will
cause you to laugh again

40.     Decree that the bands of the wicked shall be
broken asunder and their chains which have been
wrapped against you, your family, your finances will be
broken in the name of the Lord - Psalms 2:2-4

The kings of the earth set themselves, and the rulers
take counsel together, against the LORD, and against
his anointed, saying, Let us break their bands asunder,
and cast away their cords from us. He that sitteth in the
heavens shall laugh: the Lord shall have them in
derision.
Psalms 2:2-4 (KJV)

41.    Destroy every instrument of satan that devours people's prosperity in the name of the Lord - Isaiah 54:14-15

In righteousness shalt thou be established: thou shalt be far from oppression; for thou shalt not fear: and from terror; for it shall not come near thee.
Behold, they shall surely gather together, but not by me: whosoever shall gather together against thee shall fall for thy sake.
Isaiah 54:14-15 (KJV)

42.    Declare that God will beat down all those who have made themselves your enemies right before your face

43.    Release  the fire of God against every satanic abortion of dreams, visions and possibilities

44.    The  counsel  of  Herod that wants to kill the vision I am carrying will come to nothing

45.    Every project, every vision which I have initiated would reach completion in Jesus Name

46.    I boldly declare that I am a stranger to failure

47.    Satan, every of your work, plan, project intended for my hurt is rebuked in Jesus name

48.    Every distraction sent by hell will be exposed by the Lord in Jesus name

49.　Boldly declare that your inheritance is too hot for ungodly people to touch

50.　Send the fire of God to scatter the spirits that walk when men sleep - Matthew 13:25

But while men slept, his enemy came and sowed tares among the wheat, and went his way.
Matthew 13:25 (KJV)

51.　Boldly declare that your godly thoughts and expectations shall be made manifest - Proverbs 16:3

Commit thy works unto the LORD, and thy thoughts shall be established.
Proverbs 16:3 (KJV)

52.　Receive the strengthening of the Lord to complete the assignment you have started in spite of the provocation and rejection of the Sanballats and Tobias'

53.　Prophesy to your life that your hand shall be strengthened to achieve what God has placed on your heart - Nehemiah 6:9

For they all made us afraid, saying, Their hands shall be weakened from the work, that it be not done. Now therefore, O God, strengthen my hands.
Nehemiah 6:9 (KJV)

54.   Release the fire of God against every destructive spirit intended for your life's destruction

55.   Boldly declare that in spite of every opposition you shall speedily fulfil your prophetic mandate and assignment in life

56.   Break the grip of the spirit that causes much labour and little fruitfulness

57.   Pray for the deliverance from the spirit that causes people to toil without result

58.   Command the grip and bondage of life's hardship to be broken from your life

59.   Boldly declare that you are a stranger to failure

60.   Release yourself from the tendency to invest without returns - Luke 5:5

And Simon answering said unto him, Master, we have toiled all the night, and have taken nothing: nevertheless at thy word I will let down the net.
Luke 5:5 (KJV)

61.   Bind the spirit of indebtedness and command it to leave in the name of the Lord

62.   Decree result into every labour that goes forth from your hand

63. Decree that the place where you are frustrated will turn around to be the place of your celebration

64. Decree that the place where you have experienced emptiness shall become the place where you will experience provision

65. Pray for the insight that would change your life and bring a glorious transformation

66. Decree a return that shall be overflowing in every business you lay your hand on

67. Smash the gates of hell that wants to hold you down to the barest minimum

68. Every spirit that wants to abort my vision and dream shall themselves have their plans aborted

69. Every spirit that terminates vision I command them to be far from me

70. I come against every spirit that destroys the fruit of my labour

71. I release God's fire on the devourers that are trying to steal my right

72. Every attempt of the enemy to make me impoverished and broke shall meet with frustration - Judges 6:3-6

And so it was, when Israel had sown, that the
Midianites came up, and the Amalekites, and the
children of the east, even they came up against them;
And they encamped against them, and destroyed the
increase of the earth, till thou come unto Gaza, and left
no sustenance for Israel, neither sheep, nor ox, nor ass.
For they came up with their cattle and their tents, and
they came as grasshoppers for multitude; for both they
and their camels were without number: and they
entered into the land to destroy it.
And Israel was greatly impoverished because of the
Midianites; and the children of Israel cried unto the
LORD.
Judges 6:3-6 (KJV)

73.    Every fox destroying my harvest receives the fire
of God in Jesus name

74.    Every spirit of abortion intended to stop my
destiny will itself be stopped

75.    Every arrow of archers shot at me would be
met with frustration

76.    I release the fire of God against every mental
abortion, dullness of brain

77.    Every attempt of the enemy to abort my marital
vision will meet with frustration

78.    I reject and refuse every form of bankruptcy released by the spirit of death and abortion

79.    I decree that my  vision shall not experience stillbirth

80.    I boldly proclaim that my vision shall not experience rebirth failure

81.    Receive deliverance from continuous termination of your job

82.    Proclaim boldly that you are free from failure in your exams and tests

83.    Receive deliverance from working hard with no financial proof

84.    Bring the fire of God against every form of indebtedness, borrowing and deficit living

85.    In place of the spirit of abortion, increase, new vision will burst forth in your life - Isaiah 54:1-2

Sing, O barren, thou that didst not bear; break forth into singing, and cry aloud, thou that didst not travail with child: for more are the children of the desolate than the children of the married wife, saith the LORD. Enlarge the place of thy tent, and let them stretch forth the curtains of thine habitations: spare not,

lengthen thy cords, and strengthen thy stakes;
Isaiah 54:1-2 (KJV)

86.     Declare and decree that every attempt of satan to abort your calling will meet with frustration

87.     Receive the grace and power of a good finisher in the name of Jesus

88.     Receive the grace of a finisher in the name of the Lord - Philippians 2:4; 2 Timothy 4:10

Look not every man on his own things, but every man also on the things of others.
Philippians 2:4 (KJV)

For Demas hath forsaken me, having loved this present world, and is departed unto Thessalonica; Crescens to Galatia, Titus unto Dalmatia.
2 Timothy 4:10 (KJV)

89.     Every tendency, every spirit of the world that begins and doesn't finish will not rest upon your life in Jesus name

90.     Bind the spirit that forsakes its vision and forsakes people that are God-sent and command it to leave

91.     Bring the fire of God against every spirit that wants to terminate your strength and effectiveness

92. Prophesy to every dead situation, dead vision, dead dreams and begin to command a resurrection

93. Boldly declare that because your expectation is in God, it shall not be without result - Proverbs 23:18

For surely there is an end; and thine expectation shall not be cut off.
Proverbs 23:18 (KJV)

94. Declare boldly that the season of the devourer is over in your life

95. Take back everything that was stolen by the demon of devouring in the name of Jesus

96. Command restoration in every area of your life

97. Bring the fire of God against every local cankerworm, palmerworm and caterpillar

98. Anything used by the enemy to cause a devouring of your life shall meet with the fire of God

99. Every unnecessary expenses, wastage shall meet with the fire of God

100. Cut off every satanic hand that is trying to touch and destroy what belongs to you - Job 1:11

But put forth thine hand now, and touch all that he
hath, and he will curse thee to thy face.
Job 1:11 (KJV)

101. The Scriptures call the devil a thief, command a
restoration of all that he has stolen in the name of Jesus

102. Pursue and recover your blessings from every
devouring demon that has stolen from you

103. Every leakage of the pocket is commanded to
stop in your life

104. Every contrary wind that blows away your
finances must stop in Jesus Name

105. Every incidence or occurrences that devalue the
things you have worked for, command them to stop in
Jesus name

106. Build a wall of fire around all that belongs to you

107. Prophesy that you shall be fruitful in the land

108. Declare that no devourer shall be able to destroy
the fruit of your ground

109. Prophesy that every project you start will end well
- Malachi 3:11

And I will rebuke the devourer for your sakes, and he
shall not destroy the fruits of your ground; neither shall
your vine cast her fruit before the time in the field,
saith the LORD of hosts.
Malachi 3:11 (KJV)

110. Command every loss producing agent to
receive the judgement of God

111. Boldly declare that I am blessed and highly
favoured, not destroyed or under calamity - Malachi 3:10-
12

Bring ye all the tithes into the storehouse, that there
may be meat in mine house, and prove me now
herewith, saith the LORD of hosts, if I will not open
you the windows of heaven, and pour you out a blessing, that there shall not be room enough to receive it.
And I will rebuke the devourer for your sakes, and he
shall not destroy the fruits of your ground; neither shall
your vine cast her fruit before the time in the field,
saith the LORD of hosts.
And all nations shall call you blessed: for ye shall be a
delightsome land, saith the LORD of hosts.
Malachi 3:10-12 (KJV)

112. I boldly declare that in place of devouring my land
shall be delightsome

113. I boldly declare that there shall be an outpouring

of the grace and favour of God upon my life

114. Cover all your properties, investments and blessings with the blood of Jesus

115. Release blindness upon every devouring spirit that is prying into what belongs to you

116. Boldly declare that because God is your Source and Sustainer, no devil can steal what belongs to you

117. Cast down every demonic caterpillar that has come against your life

118. Cast down every demonic cankerworm that is eating the root of your property

119. Thank God because the day has come for every cloud intended to cover your glory to shift

120. Send the fire of God from His presence to devour every devourer

121. Send the fire of God from His presence to devour every thing contrary to your peace - Psalms 97:3

A fire goeth before him, and burneth up his enemies
round about.
Psalms 97:3 (KJV)

122. Prophesy that the fire of God's glory will continue to glow in your life

123. Declare boldly that sickness, barrenness, diseases and infirmity are a stranger to your destiny

124. Declare that the days of working hard and having nothing to show for it is over in your life

125. Begin to prophesy to every business you own, that the grace and strength of the Lord comes upon it

126. Declare that everything that has rendered your business and your life powerless will begin to leave in the name of Jesus

127. Boldly declare that your hands are blessed, you shall be an effective professional, business person, parent, housewife

128. Begin to pray for every inactive area of your life to begin to receive the strength of God

129. Begin to pray that every area of your life that is known for disability will begin to change to the place of your ability

# THE SPIRIT OF DELAY

1.    Thank the Lord who has proven Himself in several ways and has supplied more than you can ask for, think or pray for

2.    Cast down the spirit of delay that wants to stop you from receiving the purpose of God

3.    Take authority over the spirit of delay and procrastination that wants to hold your blessing and make you doubt God

4.    Send ministering angels to begin to retrieve every benefit, right and blessing which belongs to you which somebody is holding back

5.    Boldly declare that this is your season of divine remembrance

6.    Declare that the God who remembered Hannah would remember you

7.    Decree that the day of delay of God's Word in your life is over

8.    Confess boldly that the Word of the Lord shall not be prolonged when it will be manifest -    Ezekiel 12:28

Therefore say unto them, Thus saith the Lord GOD;
There shall none of my words be prolonged any more,
but the word which I have spoken shall be done, saith
the Lord GOD.
Ezekiel 12:28 (KJV)

9.    Go into the spirit realm and strangle every spirit of postponement that keeps your blessing away - Jeremiah 1:12

Then said the LORD unto me, Thou hast well seen: for
I will hasten my word to perform it.
Jeremiah 1:12 (KJV)

10.    Declare boldly that delay is your enemy and you have victory over it in the name of the Lord

11.    Boldly declare that you can stand to be blessed and all the blessings intended for this season shall be manifest

12.    Rebuke the spirit of delay in every area of your life and declare your fruitfulness

13.    Take   authority over barrenness caused by the spirit of delay and call forth fruitfulness

14.    Pray that everything you have already asked for in prayer will begin to gain manifestation

15.    Decree that everything God has released for this season for you in the spirit realm shall begin to have earthly manifestation

16.    Release   the   fire of God against the demons delaying your blessing, your progress, your breakthrough and your finances in the name of the Lord

17.    Every demonic aggression intended to bring hardship, difficulty and delay will meet with frustration

18.    Declare that what God is doing in your life shall before all eyes to see - Nehemiah  4:1

But it came to pass, that when Sanballat heard that we builded the wall, he was wroth, and took great indignation, and mocked the Jews.
Nehemiah 4:1 (KJV)

19.     Ask the Holy Ghost to unseat everyone occupying your rightful position

20.     Reach forth today by faith and begin to pull in all that the enemy has stolen

21.     I boldly declare that I will not wait in vain, but taste the goodness of God's favour

22.     Come   against every spirit that is producing ungodly delay in your circumstances

23.     Receive the baptism of boldness and joy in the time and seasons of waiting on God - Psalms 34:5

They looked unto him, and were lightened: and their faces were not ashamed.
Psalms 34:5 (KJV)

24.     Prophesy that your waiting will not be in vain and that you will not be put to shame

25.     Prophesy that this is your season of manifestation - Romans 8:19

For the earnest expectation of the creature waiteth for the manifestation of the sons of God.
Romans 8:19 (KJV)

# THE SPIRIT OF SEDUCTION & DECEPTION

1.    Decree that every wolf in sheep's clothing hanging around you will be exposed by the Lord

2.    Ask the Lord to open your eyes and expose every doctrine of devils intended to deceive you and make you miss the best of God

3.    Receive divine anointing to discern the voice of the enemy and to expose it

4.    Release God's fire against every scheme that wants to seduce you away from the purpose of God

5.    Decree the fire of God against every serpentine spirit

6.    I shall be beyond the reach of the seductive spirits that try to destroy precious lives

7.    Cast down every evil imagination; I tear down spirits of deception intended to mislead me; I resist every satanic provocation to do wrong - 1 Chronicles 21:1

And Satan stood up against Israel, and provoked David to number Israel.
1 Chronicles 21:1 (KJV)

8.    I release the fire of God against every satanic enticement intended to draw me away

9.    I break myself free from every ungodly soul tie I have gotten into in the name of the Lord

10.    Every Jezebel sent to entice me shall be exposed in Jesus name

11.    Every spirit of seduction intended to prevail against me shall be frustrated

12.    Every spirit of seduction intended for my affliction will meet with failure

13.   I release myself from every satanic obsession intended to drag me into sin

14.   Every wicked spirit intended to derail me from my promotion will suffer setback in Jesus name

15.   Receive the power to resist every form of seduction; sexual, financial, positional, etc

16.   Receive the power to say no to every Delilah which the enemy has assigned to you

17.   Ask the Lord to expose every lying spirit around you that is intended to deceive you

18.   Ask the Lord to open your eyes to know all the wolves around you

19.   Release the fire of God against every sorcerer, every agent of deception that may be hanging around you - Acts 8:9-11

But there was a certain man, called Simon, which beforetime in the same city used sorcery, and bewitched the people of Samaria, giving out that himself was some great one: To whom they all gave heed, from the least to the greatest, saying, This man is the great power of God. And to him they had regard, because that of long time he had bewitched them with sorceries.
Acts 8:9-11 (KJV)

20.    Confess any sin that has become an entry way for satanic oppression

21.    Every spirit that falls in love with the world is not your portion - reject it in Jesus name

22.    Everyone planted in your organisation or around you that is a instrument of devouring shall be exposed by the Lord

# THE CONTROLLING SPIRITS

## THE SPIRIT OF ALEXANDER

1.	Pray that the Holy Ghost will do justice to those who are harming your ministry

2.	Declare the power of every opposing spirit that is attacking your ministry to be null and void in the name of the Lord

3.	Come against every malicious slander raised by hell against your testimony as a minister of the gospel - 2 Timothy 4:14, 15; 1 Timothy 1:19, 20

Alexander the coppersmith did me much evil: the Lord reward him according to his works:  Of whom be thou ware also; for he hath greatly withstood our words.
2 Timothy 4:14-15 (KJV)

Holding faith, and a good conscience; which some having put away concerning faith have made shipwreck: Of whom is Hymenaeus and Alexander; whom I have delivered unto Satan, that they may learn not to blaspheme.
1 Timothy 1:19-20 (KJV)

4.     Ask the Lord to silence every fault finding spirit that is weakening the impact of your work

5.     Bring the fire of God against every opposer of good things in your life

6.     Pray that every Alexander who is bringing evil against the work God has committed to your hand will receive their just reward

7.     Receive the boldness of God to withstand those who are opposing the Word of God which you preach

8.     Command that everyone speaking blasphemy against your ministry and the work of God in your life, will be silenced by the Holy Ghost

# THE SPIRIT OF THE RICH YOUNG RULER

9.    Receive boldness to overcome every tendency of spiritual lukewarmness

10.   Receive the grace of God to silence the spirits opposing the work of God in your life

11.   Receive the grace of God to be totally committed to the cause of Christ

12.   Pray for boldness to silence every spirit of lukewarmness in your life

13.   Release God's fire against every spirit that opposes a holy zeal in your life

14.   Pray that the Holy Ghost will give you a hunger for the things of God

15.   Sever yourself free from everything that wants to draw you away from Christ

16.   Bring the fire of God against every mammon spirit

17.   Receive the grace of God that would release you and give you power to chase after Christ

18.   Reject every satanic blessing that wants to turn away your affection from God

19.     Confront the spirit that operated in Ananias and Sapphira and reject its grip on your life in Jesus name

20.     Bring the fire of God against every blasphemous spirit that wants you to lie to the Holy Ghost

21.     Bring the fire of God against every unclean spirit that wants to fill your heart with lies to the Holy Ghost

22.     Pray that every ungodly spirit that tries to conceive Satan's work in your heart would receive the fire of God

23.     Receive the grace of God to not tempt the Lord by walking in error

24.     Pray for the grace to be able to give everything when occasion demands in serving the Lord

25.     Loose yourself from the grip of a hypocritical spirit

26.     Receive the grace of God to be totally repentant and to walk in purity before the Lord

27.     Take authority over every spirit of greed and command it to leave your life in the name of Jesus - 2 Kings 5:20-27

But Gehazi, the servant of Elisha the man of God, said, Behold, my master hath spared Naaman this Syrian, in not receiving at his hands that which he brought: but, as the LORD liveth, I will run after him, and take somewhat of him. So Gehazi followed after Naaman. And when Naaman saw him running after him, he lighted down from the chariot to meet him, and said, Is all well?

And he said, All is well. My master hath sent me, saying, Behold, even now there be come to me from mount Ephraim two young men of the sons of the prophets: give them, I pray thee, a talent of silver, and two changes of garments. And Naaman said, Be content, take two talents. And he urged him, and bound two talents of silver in two bags, with two changes of garments, and laid them upon two of his servants; and they bare them before him. And when he came to the tower, he took them from their hand, and bestowed them in the house: and he let the men go, and they departed. But he went in, and stood before his master.

And Elisha said unto him, Whence comest thou, Gehazi? And he said, Thy servant went no whither. And he said unto him, Went not mine heart with thee, when the man turned again from his chariot to meet thee? Is it a time to receive money, and to receive garments, and oliveyards, and vineyards, and sheep, and oxen, and menservants, and maidservants? The leprosy therefore of Naaman shall cleave unto thee, and unto thy seed for ever. And he went out from his presence a leper as white as snow.

2 Kings 5:20-27 (KJV)

28.    Pray that everyone in your company who is there

for their greedy gain will be exposed by the Lord

29.    Pray that every ungodly jealousy directed at you will be exposed by the Lord

30.    Bind every spirit of wordliness from holding you and stopping you from doing the will of God

31.    Bring the fire of God against every spirit trying to seduce you back to worldiness

32.    Declare boldly that you will not forsake your first love for the Lord

33.    Take authority over that ungodly spirit trying to lure you with the spirit of the world

34.    Receive the grace of God not to forsake the place of your calling and commitment - 2 Timothy 4:10; Philemon 24

For Demas hath forsaken me, having loved this present world, and is departed unto Thessalonica; Crescens to Galatia, Titus unto Dalmatia.
2 Timothy 4:10 (KJV)

Marcus, Aristarchus, Demas, Lucas, my fellowlabourers.
Philemon 1:24 (KJV)

35.    Bring the fire of God against every ungodly spirit that is trying to pull you down from the heavenly place you sit with Christ

36.    Ask the Lord to open your eyes to know those to whom you are connected in your destiny and purpose

37.    Pray that your eyes will be opened to know those who will draw you away from the faith and to walk away from their tendencies

38.    Take authority over every belittling spirit that tries to say that you cannot achieve your purpose in life - Numbers 13:25 - 33; 14:1-4

And they returned from searching of the land after forty days. And they went and came to Moses, and to Aaron, and to all the congregation of the children of Israel, unto the wilderness of Paran, to Kadesh; and brought back word unto them, and unto all the congregation, and shewed them the fruit of the land. And they told him, and said, We came unto the land whither thou sentest us, and surely it floweth with milk and honey; and this is the fruit of it. Nevertheless the people be strong that dwell in the land, and the cities are walled, and very great: and moreover we saw the children of Anak there. The Amalekites dwell in the land of the south: and the Hittites, and the Jebusites, and the Amorites, dwell in the mountains: and the Canaanites dwell by the sea, and by the coast of Jordan.

And Caleb stilled the people before Moses, and said,
Let us go up at once, and possess it; for we are well
able to overcome it.  But the men that went up with
him said, We be not able to go up against the people;
for they are stronger than we.  And they brought up an
evil report of the land which they had searched unto
the children of Israel, saying, The land, through which
we have gone to search it, is a land that eateth up the
inhabitants thereof; and all the people that we saw in it
are men of a great stature. And there we saw the giants,
the sons of Anak, which come of
the giants: and we were in our own sight as
grasshoppers, and so we were in their sight.
Numbers 13:25-33 (KJV)


And all the congregation lifted up their voice, and
cried; and the people wept that night.
And all the children of Israel murmured against Moses
and against Aaron: and the whole congregation said
unto them, Would God that we had died in the land of
Egypt! or would God we had died in this wilderness!
And wherefore hath the LORD brought us unto this
land, to fall by the sword, that our wives and our
children should be a prey? were it not better for us to
return into Egypt?  And they said one to another, Let
us make a captain, and let us return into Egypt.
Numbers 14:1-4 (KJV)

39.    Receive the boldness not to let go of the
blessings earmarked for you

40.    Come against every lying spirit that compares you to a grasshopper in the face of the challenges of life

41.    Come against every lying spirit that makes you discourage other believers

42.    Receive the grace to walk in faith and not doubt and unbelief during the battles of life

43.    Declare boldly you refuse to focus on obstacles but on the promises of God

44.    Bring the fire of God against every ungodly spirit opposed to your destiny

45.    Reject and renounce the tendency to murmur in the face of the battles of life

46.    Declare that every evil report brought against God's blessing for your life will not stand in Jesus

## THE SAULISH SPIRIT - 1 SAMUEL 9:2; NUMBERS 17

And he had a son, whose name was Saul, a choice young man, and a goodly: and there was not among the children of Israel a goodlier person than he: from his shoulders and upward he was higher than any of the people.
1 Samuel 9:2 (KJV)

47.　Come against the spirit that causes leaders to fail and declare that you will not fail - 1 Samuel 15:23-24

For rebellion is as the sin of witchcraft, and stubbornness is as iniquity and idolatry. Because thou hast rejected the word of the LORD, he hath also rejected thee from being king. And Saul said unto Samuel, I have sinned: for I have transgressed the commandment of the LORD, and thy words: because I feared the people, and obeyed their voice.
1 Samuel 15:23-24 (KJV)

48.　Come against the spirit that makes you to walk under the bondage of the fear of man and not the boldness of submission to God

49.　Reject every tendency to be jealous of other people's blessing - 1 Samuel 18:8-9

And Saul was very wroth, and the saying displeased him; and he said, They have ascribed unto David ten thousands, and to me they have ascribed but thousands: and what can he have more but the kingdom?
And Saul eyed David from that day and forward.
1 Samuel18:8-9 (KJV)

50.　Take authority over every spirit that is trying to destroy and kills the vision of God in your life - 1 Samuel 20:33

And Saul cast a javelin at him to smite him: whereby
Jonathan knew that it was determined of his father to
slay David.

1 Samuel 20:33 (KJV)

51.     Reject every suicide spirit and declare your victory
over it - 1 Sam 31:4-6

Then said Saul unto his armourbearer, Draw thy sword,
and thrust me through therewith; lest these uncircum-
cised come and thrust me through, and abuse me. But
his armourbearer would not; for he was sore afraid.
Therefore Saul took a sword, and fell upon it. And
when his armourbearer saw that Saul was dead, he
fell like wise upon his sword, and died with him.
So Saul died, and his three sons, and his armourbearer,
and all his men, that same day together.

1 Samuel 31:4-6 (KJV)

52.     Bring the fire of God against every form of
witchcraft that wants to gain your attention - 1 Sam 28:1-
9

And it came to pass in those days, that the Philistines
gathered their armies together for warfare, to fight with
Israel. And Achish said unto David, Know thou
assuredly, that thou shalt go out with me to battle, thou
and thy men. And David said to Achish, Surely thou
shalt know what thy servant can do. And Achish said to
David, Therefore will I make thee keeper of mine head

for ever. Now Samuel was dead, and all Israel had lamented him, and buried him in Ramah, even in his own city. And Saul had put away those that had familiar spirits, and the wizards, out of the land.

And the Philistines gathered themselves together, and came and pitched in Shunem: and Saul gathered all Israel together, and they pitched in Gilboa. And when Saul saw the host of the Philistines, he was afraid, and his heart greatly trembled. And when Saul enquired of the LORD, the LORD answered him not, neither by dreams, nor by Urim, nor by prophets. Then said Saul unto his servants, Seek me a woman that hath a familiar spirit, that I may go to her, and enquire of her. And his servants said to him, Behold, there is a woman that hath a familiar spirit at Endor. And Saul disguised himself, and put on other raiment, and he went, and two men with him, and they came to the woman by night: and he said, I pray thee, divine unto me by the familiar spirit, and bring me him up, whom I shall name unto thee. And the woman said unto him, Behold, thou knowest what Saul hath done, how he hath cut off those that have familiar spirits, and the wizards, out of the land: wherefore then layest thou a snare for my life, to cause me to die?

1 Samuel 28:1-9 (KJV)

53.	Ask the Lord to expose to you every demonic entry point which you are not aware of

54.	Receive grace to get rid of everything that carries

a graven image and that does not glorify God in your life

55.     Receive grace to get rid of every unclean image, jewellery, or object that draws satanic attention

56.     Repent of every action that affirms foreign gods in your life - Deuteronomy 5:8

57.     Repent of your association with every ungodly image of Buddah, Hindu images, Egyptian images and Greek gods

58.     Repent of your association of the worship of the "queen of heaven"

59.     Ask the Lord to open your eyes to see wherever there is any demonic infestation in your life

60.     Command every spirit that is a leftover from false religions you were involved in to leave your life in the name of Jesus

61.     Take authority over the spirit of yoga, bahai, Christian Science, command them to leave in the name of Jesus

62.     Destroy the grip of Mormonism, Islam, Jehovah Witness, Hinduism over your life in the name of Jesus

63.     Break the grip of every unclean spirit that may

have hung onto you or your practice of false religion

64.    Bring the fire of God against every occult spirit that wants to continue in your life in the name of Jesus

65.    Command destruction on every impact, every lie of occult forces in your life

66.    Bring the fire of God against every voodoo power in your life in the name of Jesus

67.    Destroy the hold and grip of every paganistic symbol in the name of the Lord

68.    Pray that the impact of every good luck charm, astrological equipment and amulets you have touched will no longer stay in your life in the name of Jesus

69.    Declare your repentance over your association with crystal balls and other pagan symbols in the name of Jesus

70.    Bring the fire of God against every satanic mask, drums and other occult items which you have bought, touched or associated yourself with

71.    Bring the fire of God against any left over of every black magic which you may have practiced in the past

72.    Release the fire of God against every impact of

your practice of fortune-telling, palmistry, and demon worship in the name of Jesus

73.    Release the fire of God against every spirit of new age, Satanism and spirit guides which may have been associated with you

74.    Cleanse yourself with the blood of Jesus from every image, worship and practice that has an appearance of evil

75.    Cleanse yourself with the blood of Jesus and command your freedom from everything that has direct demonic influence

76.    Ask the Lord to expose to you whatever has become a supernatural master in your life and receive the power to move away from it

77.    Ask the Lord to open your eyes to know any romantic image, letter or tool of the past that is permitting the spirit of lust to come into your home

78.    Release the land under your house from previous demonic covenants in the name of Jesus

79.    Ask the Lord to reveal any bloodshed that may be causing a hindrance to prayer - Genesis 4:10-11
    And he said, What hast thou done? the voice of thy
    brother's blood crieth unto me from the ground.

And now art thou cursed from the earth, which hath opened her mouth to receive thy brother's blood from thy hand;

Genesis 4:10-11 (KJV)

80.    Break the covenant and the curses that may have come through the land on which you live or own

81.    Command every dark force inhabiting the land in which your house or property is, to leave in the name of Jesus

82.    Repent of every bloodshed that may have taken place on the land under your house

83.    Come against every spirit of violence that is still dominating the area in which you live in the name of Jesus

84.    Break every curse that has come upon your land by reason of idolatry

85.    Break every curse that may have been pronounced because of land disputes in the area where your house or property is

86.    Bring the blood of Jesus against the demonic prince over the area where your property is and command his hand off your house, your life, your land in the name of Jesus

87.   Declare   that   every   negative   occurrence, violence,   destruction, death which has been taking place in the land where you live stops in the name of Jesus

88.   Command every spirit of immorality that is still in the house or on the land in which you live to begin to leave in the name of Jesus

89.   Take authority over every wicked spirit that has been released through the practice of sin and the land which belongs to you or on which your house stands and command them to leave in the name of Jesus

90.   Welcome the presence of the Holy Spirit in your house and on that land

91.   Bring a cleansing through the Holy Ghost to the place   where   you   live   and command every spirit of darkness to loose its grip over that place in the name of Jesus

92.   Break every covenant that is evil that has been made in that house or hotel where you are staying in the name of Jesus

93.   Command the grip of the spirit of occult activity that has been practiced in the hotel room or in the place where you are staying to begin to leave in the name of Jesus

94. Receive divine impression to know what ungodly activity has taken place in the house, on the land and the hotel in which you are, and receive total breakthrough in Jesus name

95. Set your home and where you live apart for the glory of God in the name of Jesus

96. Boldly declare that your home is not a haven of darkness but the embassy of the Holy Spirit

97. Pray that your home and its surrounding will become a beacon of light to other people

98. Boldly declare to every force of darkness around your dwelling place that their time is over

99. Plead the blood of Jesus over every member of your family, your property in the name of Jesus

100. As you go through your house; room by room, prophesy the presence of the Holy Spirit in every corner of your house - Deuteronomy 7:25

The graven images of their gods shall ye burn with fire: thou shalt not desire the silver or gold that is on them, nor take it unto thee, lest thou be snared therein: for it is an abomination to the LORD thy God.
Deuteronomy 7:25 (KJV)

101. Renounce every participation of your family in

anything that brings glory to Satan and declare your freedom

102. Declare boldly that every legal right of demonic forces linked to your house or objects in your house is now broken and no longer exists

103. Declare boldly that every covenant, works of darkness no longer stands in the name of Jesus

104. Command the spirit of every negative force released in the house before you lived there; financial troubles, violence, nightmares, accidents, fighting, to begin to leave in Jesus name

105. Begin to command back every favour, blessing and joy stolen from you

106. Dedicate every room, dedicate every part of your house to the glory of God

107. Declare that the afflictions shall no longer rise now that they have been overcome

# THE SPIRITS OF ASSASSINATION

## SPIRITS OF ASSASSINATION

1.     Send the fire of God against every demonic spirit sent to assassinate you

2.     Declare that every regional spirit holding people in bondage will have no power over your life in Jesus name

3.     Every demonic spirit sent to take you out of commission will receive the fire of God in Jesus name

4.     Break the power of the spirit of assassination sent to break your family

5.      Take authority over every spirit that is trying to strangle you before your promotion and command its power broken

6.      Declare and decree that every cycle of victory and defeat turns around for total victory

7.      Every demonic spirit assigned to assassinate the joy in your marriage, receive the fire of God

8.      Every spirit assigned to destroy your finances will be frustrated in Jesus name

9.      Declare that what limited your fore-fathers will have no power over you in the name of the Lord

10.     Thank the Lord for bringing you under the bloodline and raising you beyond the power of every spirit of assassination

11.     Boldly declare that the power that limited your grandfathers and fathers will not be able to stop you

12.     Break the tentacles of every unseen force that drags you into sin

13.     Break the power of every control force in the name of Jesus

14.     Bind the spirit behind abusive relationships from holding your life

15.     Bind the spirit behind every kind of molestation from messing up with your life

16.     Break the hold of the enemy in the life of the people you are trying to win for Christ

17.     Take authority over every spirit of assassination working against the salvation of your loved ones

18.     Take authority over every spirit of assassination in the territory where you live and destroy its effect on your family

19.     Break the grip of spirits assigned to areas of your city that are causing havoc and reducing the value of the life of the people there

20.     Take authority over the spirit of alcoholism sent to assassinate you and command it to leave

21.     Break the grip of the spirit of perversion and declare that you are a free person in Jesus

22.     Send the fire of God against the spirit of assassination sent to depress you

23.     Take authority over the spirit of insanity and declare that you have a sound mind in Jesus

24.     Take authority over the spirit of violence that is ravaging society and declare that your house is a no go zone

25.     Take authority over spirits behind cycles of defeat and declare victory over them in Jesus name

26.     Pray that the Holy Ghost will expose every hidden spirit that is trying to assassinate you

27.     Take authority over every demonic entity that wants to get you off track and make you miss your way

28.     Declare that the assassination attempt of the spirit of

rape and murder will not work in your life

29.     Receive the revelation to expose every satanic assignment

30.     Ask the Lord to give you divine insight and understanding, to understand and overcome satan's devices

31.     Pray for whoever is your future spouse that whatever spirit of the assassin is assigned to them will not work

32.     Take authority over every haunting spirit sent to cause you fear in your own home and command it to leave

33.     Release spiritual bodyguards or angelic spirits around yourself in Jesus name

34.     Ask the Lord to expose everything that wants to draw you away from spiritual protection

35.     Thank the Lord for those He has assigned to be a source of spiritual protection to your life

36.     Receive the grace to discern the voice of the Lord that will expose satan's assassination attempt

37.     Send the fire of God against everything that wants to pull you away from the love of Christ and the flock of Christ

38.     Proclaim the name of the Lord Jesus Christ over your household and everything that pertains to you

39.     Declare that in the time of trouble you have taken safety and protection under the name of the Lord

40.     Ask the Lord to show you what is the weak link in your

family that is exposing you to satanic assassins

41.     Receive the grace and anointing of an intercessor, to stop the hand of the enemy from touching your house

42.     Ask the Lord to give you anointed music that will break the grip of the spirits of the assassin

43.     Declare the headship of Christ over your house

44.     Ask the Lord to uproot every seed of bitterness that becomes an entry point for spirits of assassination - Hebrews 12:15

45.     Take authority over every spirit that is trying to assassinate the testimony of your pastor

46. Destroy and counter every lie of satan intended to weaken your pastor's ministry

47.     Send the fire of God against every javelin of the devil thrown at your man of God

48. Take  authority over every unteachable spirit that wants to assassinate your joy and destiny and declare your victory over it in Jesus name - Hebrews 12:25

See that ye refuse not him that speaketh. For if they escaped not who refused him that spake on earth, much more shall not we escape, if we turn away from him that speaketh from heaven: Hebrews 12:25 (KJV)